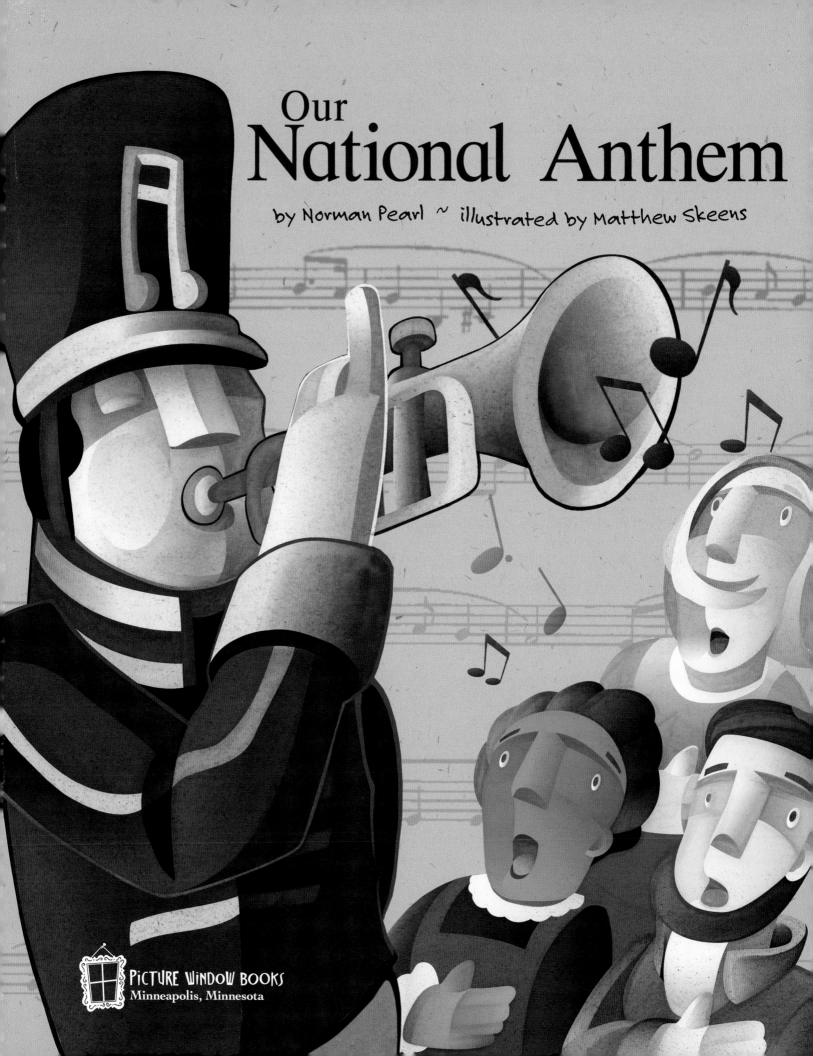

Our National Anthem

by Norman Pearl ~ illustrated by Matthew Skeens

PICTURE WINDOW BOOKS
Minneapolis, Minnesota

Special thanks to our advisers for their expertise:

Kevin Byrne, Ph.D., Professor of History
Gustavus Adolphus College

Susan Kesselring, M.A., Literacy Educator
Rosemount-Apple Valley-Eagan (Minnesota) School District

Editor: Jill Kalz
Designer: Nathan Gassman
Page Production: Tracy Kaehler and Ellen Schofield
Creative Director: Keith Griffin
Editorial Director: Carol Jones
The illustrations in this book were created digitally.
Photo credit: Library of Congress, 22, 24

Picture Window Books
5115 Excelsior Boulevard, Suite 232
Minneapolis, MN 55416
877-845-8392
www.picturewindowbooks.com

Library of Congress Cataloging-in-Publication Data
Pearl, Norman.
Our national anthem / by Norman Pearl ; illustrated by Matthew Skeens.
p. cm.—(American symbols)
Includes bibliographical references and index.
ISBN-13: 978-1-4048-2215-3 (hardcover)
ISBN-10: 1-4048-2215-1 (hardcover)
ISBN-13: 978-1-4048-2221-4 (paperback)
ISBN-10: 1-4048-2221-6 (paperback)
1. Baltimore, Battle of, Baltimore, Md., 1814—Juvenile literature. 2. United States—History—War of 1812—Flags—Juvenile literature. 3. Flags—United States—History—19th century—Juvenile literature. 4. Key, Francis Scott, 1779-1843—Juvenile literature.
5. Star-Spangled banner (Song)—Juvenile literature. I. Skeens, Matthew, ill.
II. Title. III. Series: American symbols (Picture Window Books)
E356.B2P43 2007
973.5'23097526—dc22   2006003523

Table of Contents

My name is Francis Scott Key.
I wrote the words to a very special song called
"The Star-Spangled Banner." I'm sure you've heard it.
Lots of people sing it. The song is the national anthem
of the United States. Let me tell you where the song
came from.

4

What Is a National Anthem?

A national anthem is a country's special patriotic song. By singing it, people show that they have pride in their country. Most countries have national anthems.

The U.S. flag is nicknamed the Star-Spangled Banner. *Star-spangled* means "covered with stars." *Banner* is another word for *flag*.

A Song of Freedom

The national anthem of the United States reminds Americans
of how special their country is. In many other countries,
people do not have the freedoms that Americans do.

"The Star-Spangled Banner" is a symbol of those freedoms.
Singing the national anthem makes Americans feel joined
together, or united, as a country.

Trying to Free a Friend

The story of "The Star-Spangled Banner" starts nearly 200 years ago. During the War of 1812 (1812–1815), British troops captured one of my friends, Dr. William Beanes.

During the war, Dr. Beanes had taken care of many British soldiers. Key brought letters from them to the British leaders. The letters said good things about the doctor. Key hoped the British would let Dr. Beanes go after reading the letters.

Because I was a lawyer, Dr. Beanes' neighbors asked me, Francis Scott Key, to help. The British let me and another man board the ship where Dr. Beanes was being held. We asked for his freedom.

The Attack on Fort McHenry

The British let my friend go, but we couldn't leave right away. British ships were about to attack Fort McHenry, in Baltimore Harbor. We had to stay on the ship until the battle was over.

During the night, the British attacked Fort McHenry by sea and land. These attacks were called the Battle of Baltimore.

The attack began early on September 13, 1814. The fighting lasted 25 hours. I watched the battle from the ship. Bombs filled the air with smoke. All through the night, rockets lit up the sky.

Putting the Words on Paper

My friends and I watched and wondered. Would Fort McHenry fall? By dawn, the smoke had cleared. We saw the stars and stripes of our flag flying. The United States had won!

Seeing the flag made me feel proud, so I started writing about the battle.

Fort McHenry's flag was huge. It was 42 feet (13 meters) long. That's about the length of seven grown men lying head to toe.

A Poem of Pride

I finished the poem the next day and called it "The Defense of Fort McHenry." Newspapers throughout the country printed it. I wrote four stanzas, but most people know only the first one.

The Defense of Fort McHenry

O say, can you see, by the dawn's early light,

What so proudly we hailed at the twilight's last gleaming?

Whose broad stripes and bright stars, through the perilous fight,

O'er the ramparts we watched, were so gallantly streaming?

And the rocket's red glare, the bombs bursting in air,

Gave proof through the night that our flag was still there.

O say does that star-spangled banner yet wave

O'er the land of the free, and the home of the brave?

On the shore dimly seen through the mists of the deep,

Where the foe's haughty host in dread silence reposes,

What is that which the breeze, o'er the towering steep,

As it fitfully blows, half conceals, half discloses?

Now it catches the gleam of the morning's first beam,

In full glory reflected now shines in the stream:

'Tis the Star-Spangled Banner! O long may it wave

O'er the land of the free and the home of the brave.

And where is that band who so vauntingly swore

That the havoc of war and the battle's confusion

A home and a country should leave us no more?

Their blood has washed out their foul footsteps' pollution.

No refuge could save the hireling and slave

From the terror of flight, or the gloom of the grave:

And the Star-Spangled Banner, in triumph doth wave

O'er the land of the free and the home of the brave.

O thus be it ever when freemen shall stand

Between their loved homes and the war's desolation!

Blest with vict'ry and peace, may the Heaven-rescued land

Praise the Power that hath made and preserved us a nation.

Then conquer we must when our cause it is just

And this be our motto: "In God is our Trust."

And the Star-Spangled Banner in triumph shall wave

O'er the land of the free and the home of the brave!

From Poem to Song

The poem had a note with it. People were supposed to sing the poem to an old English tune called "To Anacreon in Heaven." A man named John Stafford Smith wrote the music.

The song was sung for the first time in a Baltimore, Maryland, theater on October 19, 1814. A music store later sold the song as "The Star-Spangled Banner." Before long, everyone wanted to sing it!

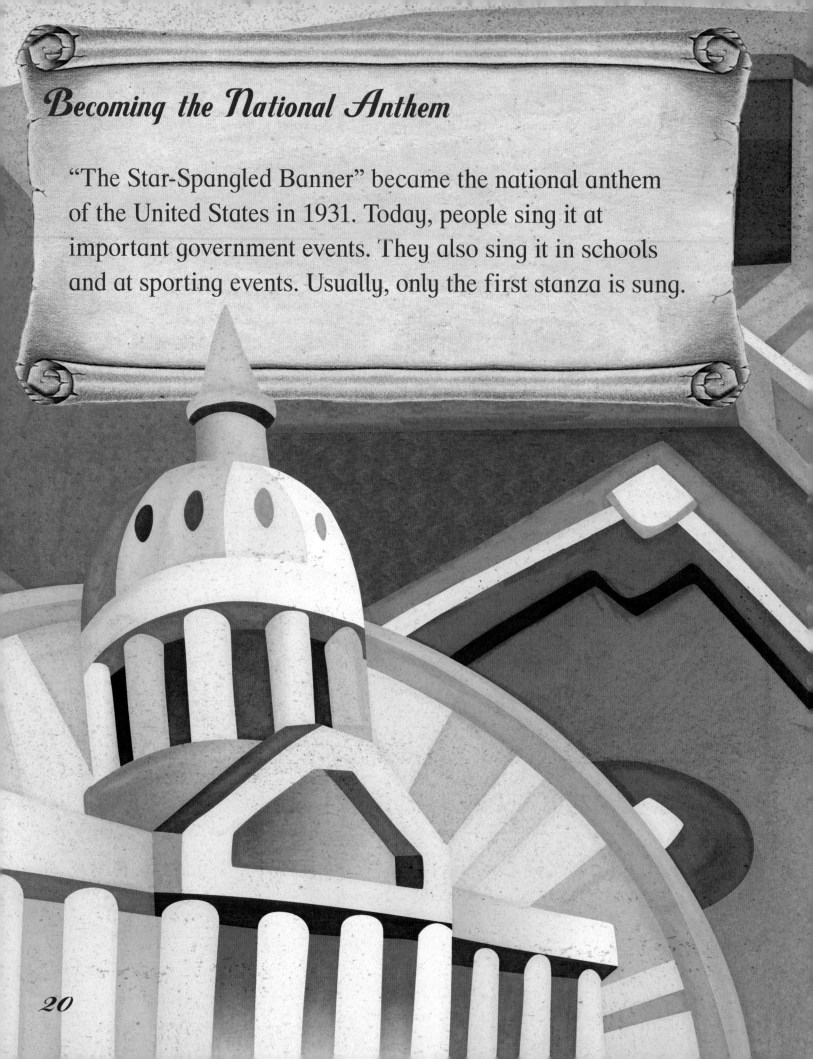

Becoming the National Anthem

"The Star-Spangled Banner" became the national anthem of the United States in 1931. Today, people sing it at important government events. They also sing it in schools and at sporting events. Usually, only the first stanza is sung.

Herbert Hoover was president when
"The Star-Spangled Banner" became
the national anthem of the United States.

That's the story of "The Star-Spangled Banner." The national anthem is one of the United States' most important symbols of freedom. Singing the song brings Americans closer together and helps them show how much they love their country.

The Star-Spangled Banner

Words by Francis Scott Key, Music by John Stafford Smith

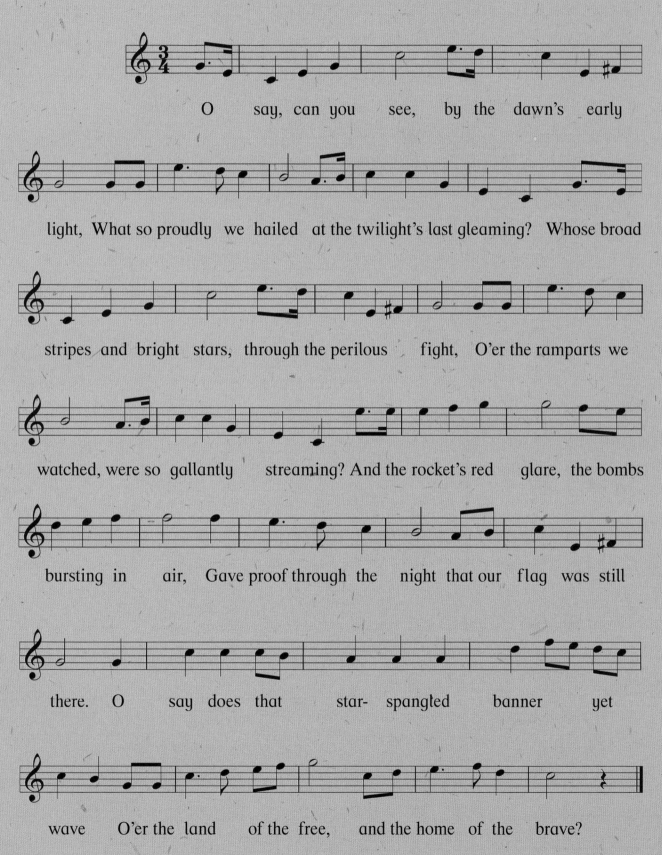

O say, can you see, by the dawn's early

light, What so proudly we hailed at the twilight's last gleaming? Whose broad

stripes and bright stars, through the perilous fight, O'er the ramparts we

watched, were so gallantly streaming? And the rocket's red glare, the bombs

bursting in air, Gave proof through the night that our flag was still

there. O say does that star- spangled banner yet

wave O'er the land of the free, and the home of the brave?

Glossary

board — to get on a ship, airplane, train, or bus

Fort McHenry — a fort in Baltimore, Maryland, that successfully defended Baltimore Harbor from the British navy in the War of 1812

patriotic — showing love for one's country

stanzas — groups of lines that are part of a poem or song

symbol — an object that stands for something else

War of 1812 — (1812–1815) a war between the United States and Great Britain over unfair British control of shipping; often called the "Second War of Independence"

The National Anthem

To Learn More

At the Library

Dell, Pamela. *The National Anthem.* Minneapolis: Compass Point Books, 2004.

Hess, Debra. *The Star Spangled Banner.* New York: Benchmark Books, 2004.

On the Web

FactHound offers a safe, fun way to find Web sites related to this book. All of the sites on FactHound have been researched by our staff.

1. Visit *www.facthound.com*
2. Type in this special code: 1404822151
3. Click on the FETCH IT button.

Your trusty FactHound will fetch the best sites for you!

Index

Look for all of the books in the American Symbols series:

The Great Seal of the United States 1-4048-2214-3
Our American Flag 1-4048-2212-7
Our National Anthem 1-4048-2215-1
The Statue of Liberty 1-4048-2216-X
The U.S. Constitution 1-4048-2643-2
The White House 1-4048-2217-8